DETECTIVE

By Dr. Eddie Vuittonet
Retired Private Special Investigator/Judge

A private detective, also known as a private investigator, is a professional hired to conduct investigations and gather information for individuals, businesses, or other organizations.

They often work independently or for private investigation agencies.

Private detectives perform various tasks, from conducting background checks to solving complex cases.

DO NOT LEARN THE HARD WAY:
The following "hint" will help protect your state license and/or keep you out of jail.

The first step in any high-crime or misdemeanor investigation is to contact the local police department to establish who the Detective in charge of the criminal case is.

The department should be able to provide the name and contact information of the Detective in charge of the case.

Once you have established contact with the Detective, discussing the scope of your involvement in the case is important.

This will help ensure your support does not impede or jeopardize the police efforts.

It is also important to establish a timeline for when the Detective will need your assistance and what type of assistance they need.

This will help to ensure that you are providing the necessary support promptly.

After meeting with the Police, you should immediately meet with your Client and brief the Client on what the Police Detective said.

Explain exactly the "rules of engagement" that the Police Detective established and to what extent your involvement in the case will be based on the meeting.

At that time, your Client can decide whether to continue or discontinue the private investigation aspect of the case.

THE FOLLOWING IS A SAMPLE OF SOME OF THE CLAUSES I INCLUDED IN MY TWO-PAGE CRIMINAL CASE CONTRACTS.

PLEASE NOTE THAT I DULY STIPULATED ABOUT MEETING WITH THE POLICE, AND BASED ON THAT MEETING, WHAT MY SERVICES WOULD BE LIMITED TO OR EXCEED AS NOT TO JEOPARDIZE ANY ONGOING POLICE INVESTIGATION OR AUGMENT IT.

This contract is made between [Name of Client] (hereinafter referred to as the "Client") and [Name of Detective] (hereinafter referred to as the "Detective").

The Client hereby engages the Detective to provide investigative services by the terms and conditions outlined in this contract.

1. Services Provided. The Detective agrees to provide the following services to the Client:
a. Conducting interviews and investigations;
b. Gathering evidence and information;
c. Analyzing evidence and information;
d. Preparing reports and other documents,
e. Providing expert testimony in court, if requested;
f. Any other services requested by the Client.
2. Payment.
a. Upon signing this contract, the Client agrees to pay the Detective a retainer fee of [amount].

b. The Detective agrees to accept half of the retainer fee up front and the other half upon the decision of the Police Detective in charge of the case, to go ahead in conjuction with his/her efforts.

REVOCABLE CRIMINAL CASE CONTRACT

Efforts to help or impede the investigation.

3. Termination. This contract may be terminated by either party at any time, with or without cause, upon written notice to the other party.

4. Confidentiality. The Detective agrees to keep all information obtained during the investigation confidential unless otherwise required by Law.

5. Indemnification. The Client agrees to indemnify and hold harmless the Detective from any claims, damages, losses, liabilities, and expenses arising out of or related to the services provided by the Detective.

6. Governing Law. This contract shall be governed by and construed by the laws of the State of [State].

IN WITNESS WHEREOF, the parties have executed this contract as of the date first written above. [Name of Client] [Name of Detective].

This contract is made between [Name of Client] (hereinafter referred to as the "Client") and [Name of Detective] (hereinafter referred to as the "Detective").

The Client hereby engages the Detective to provide investigative services by the terms and conditions outlined in this contract.

1. Contigent services to be provided.
The Detective agrees to provide the following PROJECTED services to the Client:

a. Conducting interviews and investigations;
b. Gathering evidence and information;
c. Analyzing evidence and information;
d. Preparing reports and other documents;
e. Providing expert testimony in court, if requested;
f. Any other services requested by the Client that will congruent with the Police's case-specific review, their established terms, conditions, restrictions and liberties.
g. Act as "the go-between" person in all aspects of the police progress and to establish and analyze the

"ambient temperature" of the case, i.e., if the
the case is progressing ("hot") or is at a dead-end
and is become or becoming a "cold case" that
will require further development within the
scope of (my/our) license, my coordination
with Police their continued restrictions /
liberties, and within the bounds of the laws of
the State of [State].

2. Payment. The Client agrees to pay the Detective
   a retainer fee of [amount] upon signing of this
   contract.

The Detective ETHICALLY AND LEGALLY agrees to accept
ONLY half of the UNREFUNDABLE retainer fee OF:
$_____________ upfront
AND..................
The other half OF $____________ is contingent, in part, upon
the decisions(s) of the Police Detective in charge of the case,
specifically on what my limitation and liberties should be that
he/she determines will help and not impede the "ongoing" or
"open" investigation.

3. Again—Termination. Either party may terminate this
contract at any time, with or without cause, upon written notice
to the other party.

No phone calls, emails, internet chats, or texts will be acceptable
for terminating this contract.

4. Confidentiality. The Detective agrees to keep all information
obtained during the investigation confidential unless otherwise
required by Law.

5. Indemnification. The Client agrees to indemnify and hold harmless the Detective from any claims, damages, losses, liabilities, and expenses arising out of or related to the services provided by the Detective.

6. Governing Law. This contract shall be governed by and construed by the laws of the State of [State].

Add more clauses to meet your needs and ensure that you stipulate how much you will charge an hour or day, mileage, and per diem charges beyond the amount of time and expenses your retainer will initially cover.

I became a licensed Private Investigator in Texas in 1985 at 34.
Before that, I was a private investigator in Toledo, Ohio, when I was
only 20.

However, I was quickly released from the job because I was not 21
years old.

My service was short-lived; however, one assignment impeded a 50-
year career.

By 25, I was a karate instructor and youth development specialist for the City of Fresno's Community Development Department.

I utilized my job position to provide local Police with pertinent information on gang members and gang activity and used this job experience to garner a Private Investigation license.

I embarked on numerous investigations showcasing surveillance skills, gathering evidence, and essentially any legal means in uncovering the truth.

Here are but a very few scenarios highlighting some of my notable cases:

I was investigating well before the "paralegal investigator" or office investigator existed.

Here are some of the duties and responsibilities an attorney's employee has.

The in-house official paralegal or office investigator is responsible for researching legal documents, gathering evidence, and preparing legal documents for an attorney he works with.

He also organizes and maintains legal files and prepares reports for the attorney.

He may also be responsible for interviewing witnesses and preparing legal briefs.

The in-house paralegal at Imes works independently and should have excellent communication and organizational skills.
He works with various people, including attorneys, private investigators, Police, clients, and other legal professionals.

HINT:
ALWAYS ADVISE YOUR CLIENT AND/OR THEIR ATTORNEY ABOUT THE FOLLOWING FACTS AS A MEANS TO CAPTURE MORE CONTRACTS AND INCREASE YOUR REVENUE. (MONEY)

As a private investigator, you can provide a more comprehensive investigation than a paralegal investigator.

As a private investigator, you can access more resources and databases and conduct in-depth interviews and background checks.

As a private investigator, you can also provide better surveillance services after working hours, which can be invaluable in certain cases.

As a private investigator, you can also provide expert, third-party, unbiased testimony in court, which can greatly assist a case.

The Suspicious Spouse

I often encountered what I called "The Suspicious Spouse."

This is something you might consider:
When a potential client approaches you, suspecting their spouse of infidelity, they usually provide you with limited information and what they believe is a schedule of their partner's daily activities.

Prepare to dedicate weeks to conducting Surveillance, discreetly following the spouse's movements, and capturing photographic evidence.

Through your efforts, you can catch the spouse meeting with a secret lover, ultimately providing irrefutable evidence to your Client.

The Triggers:
The wife notices her husband's behavior has changed drastically in the past few weeks.

He is distant and distracted and often stays out late without explanation.

He has become secretive and evasive when she asks him questions, and he has started to dress differently.

He has also become increasingly distant and withdrawn from their marriage.

The wife is suspicious of her husband's behavior and begins to suspect that he is having an affair.

She starts to look for clues and evidence that might confirm her suspicions.

She notices he has received strange phone calls and texts late at night.

He also seems to be spending more time away from home and is often seen in the company of another woman.

The wife decides to hire you to find out the truth.

She hopes that the investigator will be able to uncover the identity of the other woman or even if her husband is involved in a homosexual relationship.

She is determined to find the truth and is willing to do whatever it takes to investigate the situation.

The following is a short story I wrote regarding one of my cases.

Unraveling Secrets
"A Riveting Tale of Betrayal and Redemption!"
In a gripping tale of deception and determination, a divorce attorney's quest for evidence takes an unexpected turn, leading to an astonishing discovery.

Follow along as we delve into the story of one investigator's encounters and the unveiled explosive secrets.

Deep within the realms of the complicated world of marital disputes, hidden truths often lurk.

Such was the case when a capable divorce attorney sought me to collect evidence to support his Client's claims of her husband's infidelity.

Little did I know that my journey would become a rollercoaster ride of unexpected encounters and heart-pounding moments.

On a day like any other, the attorney's Client found herself amid a crucial exchange.

A court order required her to hand over her little girl to her soon-to-be ex-husband.

The attorney, sensing an opportunity to validate her Client's allegations, hired me to watch the Client's husband's every move closely.

One day, as I followed the unsuspecting man across town, fate dealt me an unexpected blow—an encounter with an irate older man who wanted me to move my car because he claimed I was at the street curb where he parked.

This unexpected interaction temporarily thwarted my mission. It forced me to regroup and find a new surveillance location because his screaming would have drawn "my mark's" attention, in turn blowing my cover.

With my resilience intact, I waited for my mark to exit the apartment.

When he did, I cautiously pursued my target and ultimately found myself in a quiet community several miles away from the city.

Positioned afar, I finally secured a vantage point behind my mark's property.

A thinly wooded area separated us, providing me with cover and a clear line of sight.

Just as the stars seemed aligned in my favor, an unmarked federal officer's DEA car appeared out of nowhere, demanding an explanation of my presence.

Caught off guard, I cautiously revealed the nature of my investigation.

To my astonishment, the officer informed me that the man I was observing was reputed to be a notorious drug dealer and that I should be very careful and leave as soon as possible.

The situation unexpectedly twisted when the man's alleged lover arrived in her car, seemingly confirming the attorney's Client's suspicions.

As my mark stepped outside to embrace his partner warmly, I seized the moment, capturing damning evidence using my trusty long-lens 35mm camera.

Sometimes, an investigation may take unexpected turns, revealing more than anticipated.

This twist-filled story reminds us that even amidst chaos, justice can still prevail, sooner or later; however, ensure you remain alive to discuss it.

The Missing Heir

A wealthy client may seek your assistance locating a missing person entitled to a significant inheritance.

Armed with several leads, you must tirelessly investigate their background, cross-referencing records and conducting interviews.

Your persistent efforts will eventually pay off when you discover the missing heir living incognito in a remote town, having assumed another identity to escape their troubled past.

When a recently deceased son or daughter needs to finalize their will but cannot find their sibling, they may need to enlist the help of a private investigator.

A private investigator can use their resources and expertise to locate a missing person.

Private investigators have access to databases and other resources that can help them locate a missing person.

They can also use their investigative skills to track down a missing person.

Private investigators can also help the recently deceased person's son or daughter by providing them with information about the missing sibling.

They can provide background information, such as where the missing sibling lived, worked, or attended school.

This information can help the descendants determine if the missing sibling is still alive and if they are still in contact with family members.

Private investigators can also help the recently deceased survivors by providing them with information about the missing sibling's financial situation.

This investigation can help the child of the recently deceased person determine if the missing sibling has any assets that need to be distributed in the will.

Private investigators can also provide information about the missing sibling's legal status, such as if they have any outstanding debts or legal issues that need to be addressed.

Finally, private investigators can help the recently deceased person' child by providing them with information about the missing sibling's current whereabouts.

Private investigators can use their resources to locate the missing sibling and provide the relatives with their current address.

This process can help the recently deceased person contact the missing sibling and finalize the probate process.

A CASE I WORKED ON

THE THREE WILLS OF JANE (Name Changed)
A Cautionary Tale
Stories of betrayal and deception can often leave us feeling disheartened and questioning the true intentions of those around us.

Today, I want to highlight a heartbreaking case highlighting the importance of vigilance and protecting our loved ones from scams.

This story involves Jane, an older woman, and a manipulative scammer named Pearl, who weaves a web of deceit to claim Jane and half her husband's fortune.

As a young investigator in the 1980s, I was approached by a wealthy older man who had seen through this scammer's wicked plans.

This unscrupulous individual had disguised herself as a caring friend to the unsuspecting Jane, plotting to take advantage of her age and vulnerability.

Pearl, driven by greed, had set her sights on a large leather bag filled with over a quarter million dollars in cash, among other things.

Jane innocently told the scammer that her husband had amassed this wealth from his successful motel business and had hidden the cash in a bag in their closet.

Seizing an opportunity when my Client was away, the scammer orchestrated a cunning theft of the bag and succeeded.

In the interim, Pearl drafted a will and fooled Jane into signing it, assigning her as her beneficiary to half of Jane's possessions and the motel as her own.

But the older man was not easily fooled.

He discovered and revoked the initial will, disrupting Pearl's plans.

Unwilling to surrender, the scammer devised an elaborate scheme, drafting a second will with the same intentions.

However, her deceitfulness was overruled once more, as the older man discovered her plot and revoked the will again.

Meanwhile, Jane's health began to decline, and she found herself confined to a hospital bed.

This presented an opportune moment for the scammer, who cunningly enticed Jane with copious amounts of orange juice, knowing full well about her hyperkalemia condition.

As Jane lay weak and vulnerable, Pearl seized the opportunity, producing a third will in which she named herself the sole beneficiary.

With a few nurses serving as witnesses, she manipulated Jane into signing against her best interests.

Tragically, Jane's life ended a few hours later that night under the influence of a manipulative scammer who exploited her trust and frailty.

This story underscores the importance of recognizing the signs of fraud and safeguarding ourselves and our loved ones from unscrupulous individuals seeking personal gain.

The means and methods that I employed to solve the case:

I gathered enough evidence to track down the thief and a portion of the money by calling the suspect's ex-wife under the pretext that I was from Publishers Warehouse and was trying to locate her ex-husband to present his 50,000-dollar cash prize.

I obtained his address and phone number in a "New York Minute" because they had a minor child in common.

Under Texas law, she could petition the court to modulate her monthly child support to reflect her x's cash windfall.

With that key information, I gathered the evidence I had developed.

I handed my Client's attorney the depositions, interviews, fingerprints, and other pertinent incriminating evidence.

The Police were called (after the fact), and a police report was garnered a few days later.

The police chief immediately ended his investigation after he reviewed my notes, interviews, and fingerprint cards (which he took).

After that, I handed the County District Attorney "the package."

He reviewed it and gave the green light to obtain an arrest warrant through a magistrate.

Incidentally, the DA was so impressed with my work that he offered me a job as a (peace officer) special investigator.

The Police in Dallas were contacted, located the suspect, and arrested him.

He was subsequently brought down for prosecution.

The Dallas police department retrieved a little less than half the money, indicating that he and Pearl had split the stash 50%;

however, he never "turned" on the scammer and took 100% of the responsibility.

The District Attorney did not choose to prosecute Pearl partly because of politics.

The scammer was a prominent business lady with high-ranking friends.

We received the following finding memorandum from the Attorney General's office of the State of Texas.

That was the impetus for the County DA to choose not to prosecute!

Subject: Understanding and Establishing Criminal Elements for Successful Prosecutions

This memorandum reminds all prosecutors of the importance of understanding and establishing criminal elements for successful prosecutions.

It is essential to accurately interpret and prove criminal elements to ensure fair and just prosecution.

As the legal system continues to evolve, so does the interpretation and proof of criminal elements.

It is, therefore, essential that prosecutors stay current on the latest developments to ensure successful prosecutions.

We were disappointed, to say the least, but we pulled our resources together and concentrated on the civil case.

Nonetheless, we successfully contested the will, deeming it invalid based on coercion, mental status, and criminal intent, and were awarded $125,000. (which I got 10% of) and the attorney receives 40%.

That was pretty keen because I had been billing at $35.00 an hour, sometimes 9 to 10 hours daily, and made over $30,000 in a matter of weeks…and 10% of the gross amount of the civil case award.

HINT:
Always have an optional clause in your Client Services Contract to garner above and beyond your total fees.

Taking on cases solely on a "contingent basis " is never a good idea. "

Always get a retainer fee that covers your projected hours and preliminary out-of-pocket expenses such as "snitch fees," travel, and meals.

Always explain the retainer fee, your projected hours, and the per dium fee.

Half of the retainer should be proportional to the services you will provide; it will only go further if the remaining balance is paid within five days!

Remember, If the case involves criminality, you must speak to the police detective in charge or report the crime before the rest of the retainer is paid by the Client, by you having to spring the bad news.

The ground rules will be established, and you can relate to your Client what you WILL DO and CAN'T DO regarding the

ACTIVE police investigation.

A **COLD CASE** can be predicated differently; you can do whatever you can do within the scope of your license or advice of the Police and not be tagged for police interference, obstruction of justice, and/or impersonating a peace officer.

After speaking to the Police, your Client may no longer want to use you... explain just why, where, when, and how you need it.

You can always "play hardball" with your Client and demand the rest of the retainer, never disclosing that you only worked enough to congruent with 1/2 the retainer.

You can always gain more revenue by asking for more hours if the case needs more development!

Hold your preliminary report at your office until you have been paid; however, by State Law, a request for a report requires a full report of the case to be handed over ASAP.

HINT:
In a Civil Action, you have full control of the investigation, whereas in a criminal case, you don't; however, in both types, you must ensure that you always remain a key, indispensable player in the case if you stick to the scope of your license, demonstrate keen logic, exude knowledge, dress for the occasion, and maintain a great work ethic.

Here is a sample of an optional clause, often called a "cherry on top of a pie option."

If the Client doesn't want to cut you in, don't push the issue and lose the case because of that!

Clause:
When the case is brought to civil court, the Client agrees to pay me, the Private Investigator (Developer), a ____% fraction of the award(s).

The Information Thief

Watch out for "snitches."

A large corporation, small business, or even a gamer may approach you, suspecting that sensitive information is being leaked to competitors, neighbors, relatives, lovers, or identity thieves.

My experience has been that clients usually provide little evidence; thus, you must delve deep into your "war bag" and find your most expensive investigative tools to employ sophisticated surveillance techniques to monitor the activities of computer keystrokes, internet and intranet usage, electronic bugs, and dishonest people.

Through careful analysis and an undercover operation, you will develop your case and expose the employee or group of employees who are gifting or selling confidential information to a store, person, club, or rival company, ultimately saving the Client from potential financial or personal information losses.

Hiring a private investigator to identify who is stealing intellectual property, proprietary formulas, or receipts is important in protecting a business's assets.

Private investigators are trained to conduct investigations discreetly and professionally and have access to resources and technology to help them uncover the thief's identity.

Private investigators can also provide valuable insight into thief methods, which can help the business take steps to prevent future thefts.

Private investigators can also help businesses identify the source of the stolen property.

They can use surveillance techniques to track the thief's movements and determine where the stolen property is being taken.

This type of investigation can help the business determine if the thief is working alone or if they are part of a larger criminal organization.

Finally, private investigators can help businesses recover stolen property.

They can use their resources to locate the stolen property and return it to the rightful owner.
This process can help the business recoup some of the losses associated with the theft and protect its intellectual property in the future.

The Property Thief

Human Rat:
A person, organization, or business can hire you to recover stolen property that has been missing for years or recently stolen.

Your investigation can lead to a criminal underworld filled with art forgeries, fencers, criminal enterprises, gangs, and acts of illicit traders.

Kleptomania (klep-toe-MAY-nee-uh) is defined as an individual with a mental health disorder that involves repeatedly being unable to resist urges to steal items that they generally don't need.

Often, the items stolen have little value, and you could afford to buy them. Kleptomania is rare but can be a serious condition.

Attempting to profit from the stolen item remains one of the biggest giveaways that the accused person may not have kleptomania.

Britannica says kleptomaniacs rarely put their stolen items to personal or profitable use.

Instead, they may even try to return the product. Others give them away or hide them.

In fact, most kleptomaniacs have the financial means to pay for the goods they steal.

Unfortunately, even with treatment, no cure exists for kleptomaniacs.

Even so, with continued sessions of psychotherapy, kleptomaniacs may uncover the reasons behind the thrill of the steal and learn to control their impulses.

You may oftentimes have to go "undercover."

After gaining a criminal's trust, you can develop the necessary information to uncover the stolen location and who stole the property.

This information can help law enforcement recover stolen merchandise and return it to its rightful owner.

A detective should take a few precautions when entering a warehouse or apartment to view stolen merchandise and arrest the thief.

First, the Detective should ensure they are properly equipped with protective gear, such as a bulletproof vest, helmet, and other protective clothing.

The Detective should also make sure that at least one other officer accompanies them, as this will provide additional safety and security.

The Detective should also be aware of their surroundings and note any suspicious activity.

They should also know potential escape routes and be prepared to act quickly.

Additionally, the Detective should be prepared to use any necessary force to apprehend the thief.

Finally, the Detective should be aware of any potential evidence in the warehouse or apartment.

This investigation could include stolen merchandise, documents, or other items that could be used as evidence in court.

The Detective should take the necessary steps to collect and secure any evidence that is found.

A private investigator approaching a band of thieves in a structure to arrest them is essentially a private citizen's arrest.

A private investigator's citizen arrest differs from a peace officer's in several ways.

A private investigator is not a law enforcement officer and does not have the same authority as a peace officer.

A private investigator is a private citizen with the right to arrest a citizen if they witness a crime being committed.

A private investigator can only make an arrest if they have witnessed the crime or have probable cause to believe that it has been committed.

On the other hand, a peace officer has the authority to arrest without having witnessed the crime being committed.

A peace officer can arrest based on probable cause or a warrant. A peace officer also has the authority to use force to make an arrest if necessary.

In addition, a private investigator's citizen arrest is limited to the State in which they are licensed.

A peace officer, however, has the authority to arrest in any jurisdiction.

Overall, the distinction between a private investigator's citizen arrest and that of a peace officer is clear.

Private investigators have limited authority to make arrests and are licensed only in the State where they operate.

Peace officers, however, can arrest in any jurisdiction and use force if necessary.

The Insurance Fraud

Insurance fraud is a serious problem affecting insurance companies and the general public.

Insurance fraud can take many forms, from false claims to identity theft.

Insurance companies are particularly vulnerable to fraud because they rely on their customers' honesty to report their losses and damages accurately.

One of the most common ways insurance companies are defrauded is through false claims.

This type of fraud occurs when a person claims a loss or damage that did not occur.

This can be done by exaggerating the extent of the damage or by making up a claim altogether.

False claims can be difficult to detect, often involving complex paperwork and documentation.

Another way that insurance companies are defrauded is through identity theft.

This type of fraud occurs when someone uses someone else's personal information to obtain insurance coverage or make a claim.

Identity theft can be difficult to detect, as the perpetrator may use a false name or address to make the claim.

Finally, insurance companies can be defrauded through the use of staged accidents.

This type of fraud occurs when two or more people conspire to create a false accident to make a claim.

Staged accidents can be difficult to detect, often involving multiple people and vehicles.

Insurance fraud is a serious problem affecting insurance companies and the general public.

Insurance companies must take steps to protect themselves from fraud, such as conducting thorough background checks on potential customers and implementing a fraud detection system.

Insurance companies can help protect themselves from fraud by taking these steps and ensuring that their customers are treated fairly.

Worker's Compensation:
Private investigators are often hired to investigate workers' compensation fraud.

This type of fraud occurs when an individual attempts to receive benefits from a workers' compensation program by faking a job-related injury or disability claim.

Private investigators can use various means and methods to fraudulently catch a person receiving workers' compensation.

One of the most common methods used by private investigators is Surveillance.

Private investigators can conduct Surveillance of the individual in question to determine if they are engaging in activities inconsistent with their reported injury or disability.

This can include activities such as driving, lifting heavy objects, or engaging in physical activities that would be difficult or impossible for someone with the reported injury or disability.

Private investigators can also interview the individual's coworkers, friends, and family members to determine whether they know about the individual's activities.

This can help to uncover any inconsistencies in the individual's reported injury or disability.

In addition, private investigators can conduct background checks on individuals to determine whether they have a history of filing false workers' compensation claims.

This can help uncover any fraud patterns that the individual may have engaged in in the past.

Finally, private investigators can also obtain records from the individual's employer to determine if they have received any payments or benefits for a job-related injury or disability.

This can help uncover discrepancies between the individual's reported injury or disability and their actual payments or benefits.

An insurance company may suspect a claimant of falsely exaggerating their injuries to receive a significant payout.

Using your knowledge of surveillance techniques, you will monitor the claimant's activities and document their daily routines and physical capabilities.

With a thorough analysis of the gathered evidence, you will prove that the individual was indeed committing insurance fraud, ensuring their claim was denied and protecting the company from financial loss.

These cases represent just a fraction of the challenging scenarios you encounter as a licensed private investigator.

Slip and Fall:

A private investigator would investigate a slip-and-fall scammer by gathering evidence.

This could include surveillance footage from the fall scene, witness statements, and other relevant information.

The investigator would then analyze the evidence to determine if the fall was a scam.

If the evidence suggests that the fall was a scam, the investigator would investigate the scammer's background.

This could include looking into their financial records, past criminal activity, and other relevant information.

The investigator would also look into the circumstances of the fall.

This could include examining the area where the fall occurred, the type of surface, and any other factors that could have contributed to the fall.

Finally, the investigator would look into the motives of the scammer.

This could include looking into their financial situation, potential benefits they may have received from the fall, and other relevant information.

By gathering and analyzing all of this evidence, the investigator could determine if the fall was indeed a scam.

Other Common Scams: Automotive

1. **Odometer Fraud: Odometer fraud is among the most common car scams.**

It involves tampering with a vehicle's odometer to make it appear like the car has fewer miles than it does.

This can be done by rolling back the odometer or disconnecting it altogether.

2. **Lemon Law Scams:** Lemon law scams involve selling a car deemed a "lemon" by a manufacturer.

These cars have a history of mechanical problems and are unsafe to drive.

The seller may try to hide this fact by not disclosing the car's history or providing false information about the car's condition.

3. **Title Washing:** Title washing is a scam that involves altering a car's title to make it appear as though the car has a clean title when it has a salvage title.

This can be done by changing the title or transferring it to another state.

4. **Fake Car Ads:** Fake car ads are a type of scam that involves posting a fake advertisement for a car that does not exist.

The seller may try to get the buyer to send money for the car without ever actually delivering the car.

5. **Unlicensed Dealers:** Unlicensed dealers are another type of car scam.

These dealers may try to sell cars without a valid license or the proper paperwork.

They may also try to sell cars that have been stolen or are not roadworthy.

The Meat and Potatoes:

Private investigators specialize in gathering information and evidence for their clients.

They use various techniques to uncover the truth, depending on the nature of the investigation.

Private investigators can be hired to investigate various matters, including criminal activity, infidelity, missing persons, and fraud.

One of the most common techniques used by private investigators is Surveillance.

Surveillance involves using cameras, audio recording devices, and other technology to observe and record a person or group's activities.

Private investigators may also use undercover operations to gather evidence.

This involves posing as someone else to gain access to information or to observe a person or group.

Another technique used by private investigators is interviewing. Private investigators may interview witnesses, suspects, or victims to gain information or verify facts.

 Private investigators may also use public records searches to uncover information about a person or group.

This may include searching for criminal records, property records, or other public documents.

Private investigators may also use computer forensics to uncover evidence.

This involves using specialized software to analyze data on computers, phones, and other digital devices.

Private investigators may also use social media to uncover information about a person or group.

This may include searching for posts, photos, and other information that can provide insight into a person's activities or intentions.

The value and significance of hiring a private investigator can vary depending on the nature of the investigation.

Private investigators can provide valuable information and evidence to be used in court or to resolve disputes.

They can also provide peace of mind to individuals who are concerned about the safety of their family or property.

Private investigators can also help uncover the truth in cases where the facts are unclear or where there is a lack of evidence.

Surveillance:

Surveillance is a private detective's most important technique.

This involves discreetly observing and documenting the activities and behaviors of a subject.

Surveillance can be conducted using various methods such as physical observation, video recording, or specialized equipment like hidden cameras or GPS tracking devices.

It helps gather evidence or monitor the activities of individuals involved in a case.

The following delineates twelve basic surveillance techniques utilized by a PI.

Physical observation:

Physical observation involves observing the subject's movements, activities, and behaviors without their knowledge.

Detectives may use binoculars, disguises, or stakeouts to gather information.

When private investigators passively observe a person, they employ several basic techniques to gather information.

These techniques include:

Stakeout:
A private investigator may conduct Surveillance from a discreet location to observe an individual's activities and behavior.

Detectives must be more inconspicuous, using binoculars, cameras, or other surveillance equipment to collect visual evidence.

A detective typically follows a specific process to identify a stakeout location, prepare for the stakeout, and effectively use surveillance equipment.

Here's a step-by-step breakdown of the process:
Gathering information:

Before initiating a stakeout, the Detective conducts thorough research to gather as much information as possible about the individual they observe.

Information may include their daily routine, frequently visited places, and potential patterns or habits.

Identifying a stakeout location:

The Detective selects a suitable location based on the gathered information.

This location should offer a discreet vantage point that allows unobstructed views of the individual's activities while ensuring the Detective remains inconspicuous.

Be aware of your surroundings:
Develop strong situational awareness to identify suspicious activities or unfamiliar individuals during your investigations.

Situation awareness will help you detect potential countersurveillance efforts.

Use a mix of covert and overt techniques:
Alter your investigative techniques to include covert (secretive) and overt (visible) methods.

Constantly relying on covert methods may raise suspicion, so utilizing overt approaches can help blend in and reduce the likelihood of countersurveillance.

Vary your routines:
Establishing predictable patterns can make it easier for countersurveillance teams to identify and track you.

By varying your routines, such as changing your routes, timings, or modes of transportation, you can make it more difficult for anyone tailing you.

Maintain communication protocols:
Establish secure protocols to protect sensitive information.

Encrypted communication apps or secure channels can help prevent eavesdropping or interception of communication.

Stay cautious with technology:
Be vigilant when using electronic devices, as they can be
compromised or used for tracking.

Check for signs of tampering regularly, use strong passwords,
enable encryption, and consider using dedicated, secure devices
for sensitive communications.

Conduct countersurveillance activities:
Occasionally, employ your techniques to identify and deter
potential threats.

Countersurveillance can involve monitoring suspicious vehicles
or individuals, conducting background checks, or using
technical surveillance countermeasures (TSCM) to detect
hidden surveillance devices.

Build a Network:

Develop connections with trusted professionals, such as lawyers or other investigators, who can provide guidance on legal matters and help protect your interests.

Collaborating with experienced colleagues can give you valuable insights into countersurveillance tactics and strategies.

Remember, the techniques to avoid countersurveillance will depend on your jurisdiction's circumstances and legal limitations.

Consulting with seasoned investigators and legal professionals will provide you with more comprehensive guidance tailored to your situation.

Preparation:

The Detective prepares for the stakeout by bringing the necessary equipment, including binoculars, a long-lens camera, a laptop, or a tablet.

They ensure all equipment works properly and have additional batteries or power sources if needed.

They may also carry a notebook or recording device to document any observations.

Disguise and inconspicuousness:
The Detective dresses appropriately for the location and time of day to remain inconspicuous.

They avoid attracting attention and blend in with their surroundings.

Disguises and props may be used as necessary, depending on the circumstances.

Setting up surveillance equipment:
The Detective set up their equipment at the stakeout location.

The setup process may involve positioning the long-lens camera to capture clear and close-up visuals from a safe distance.

Additionally, they may set up a laptop or tablet for live monitoring or recording purposes.

Observation:
The Detective observes the individual once everything is in place.

They use binoculars to enhance their view and actively monitor their activities if necessary.

The Detective should be patient and attentive, documenting any significant or suspicious behavior as it occurs.

Collecting evidence:

Throughout the stakeout, the Detective uses their cameras or recording devices to collect visual evidence, capturing photographs or video footage of any relevant activities.

This evidence can be critical for supporting or disproving claims or suspicions.

Maintaining communication:

Sometimes, a detective might have a team working with them during a stakeout.

In such situations, it's important to maintain discreet communication to relay observations or coordinate actions effectively.

Secret communication can be done via encrypted communication devices or other secure methods.

Note-taking:
During passive observation, the private investigator maintains detailed notes and records of all observations made during the investigation.

These notes are vital for accurate reporting, analysis, and potential legal purposes.

Documentation:
Private investigators may document the subject's activities using photographs or videos.

These documents serve as evidence to support their findings and reports.

Reporting:
After each observation session, the private investigator compiles a thorough report summarizing their findings.

The report typically includes the date, time, location, and descriptions of events, activities, and interactions observed.

Behavior analysis:
A private investigator keenly observes the subject's behavior, body language, and interactions with others.

This analysis helps conclude the subject's motives, character, or potential involvement in certain activities.

Vehicle tracking:
 In cases where the subject frequently travels by car, a private investigator may discreetly attach a tracking device to the vehicle to monitor their movements remotely.

This information can be valuable in establishing patterns or identifying potential affiliations.

Covert recording:
Depending on the jurisdiction's legal regulations, a private investigator may use hidden audio or video recording devices to capture conversations or activities that could be crucial to the investigation.

Remember, the techniques and equipment utilized during a stakeout may vary depending on the situation, location, and legal restrictions.

Detectives must always adhere to local laws and regulations governing Surveillance and privacy to ensure their actions remain valid and ethically sound.

It is important to note that private investigators must operate within their profession's legal boundaries and ethical guidelines.

Surveillance, documentation, and evidence collection laws vary, so investigators must ensure their actions comply with applicable regulations.

Methods and Means:

Private detectives may use cameras to record video footage of the subject's activities.

Video recording can be done using hidden, body-worn, or surveillance systems installed in public areas.

Private detectives may take discreet photographs of the subject in various situations to gather evidence or document their activities.

Photography can be done using telephoto lenses or concealed cameras.

GPS Tracking:
Private detectives may use tracking devices or GPS technology to monitor the subject's real-time movements.

These devices can be discreetly placed on vehicles or personal belongings.

Electronic Surveillance involves using specialized equipment to monitor and record the subject's electronic communications, such as phone calls or internet activities.

Private detectives may use wiretaps, computer monitoring software, or hacking techniques (subject to legal restrictions).

Undercover Operations:
Private detectives may assume false identities or go undercover to gain access to information or gather evidence.

This technique requires the Detective to blend in with the subject's environment without arousing suspicion.

Background Checks: Detectives may conduct detailed investigations into a subject's personal, professional, and financial background to gather relevant information.

A "BC" check can involve searching public records, interviewing sources, or verifying credentials and references.

Open Source Intelligence (OSINT): Private detectives gather information about a subject using publicly available information from social media, news articles, or public records.

Interviewing Witnesses:
Detectives may interview individuals with knowledge or information about the case.

An interview can be done discreetly to prevent the subject from becoming aware of the investigation.

Surveillance Equipment:

Private detectives may use specialized surveillance equipment such as listening devices, hidden cameras, long-range lenses, or night vision equipment to facilitate their investigations.

Vehicle Tracking: Detectives may use tracking devices to monitor the subject's movements when driving a vehicle.

Vehicle tracking can provide valuable information about their whereabouts and activities.

Data Analysis:
Private detectives may analyze large amounts of data, such as financial records, phone records, or internet usage, to identify patterns, associations, or anomalies that can be used to gather evidence or build a case.

It is important to note that the legality and ethical use of these surveillance techniques can vary depending on jurisdiction.

Private detectives must adhere to local laws and regulations while conducting their investigations.

Background checks:
Private detectives often conduct comprehensive background checks on individuals.

They gather information about the person's personal history, criminal records, education, employment, financial status, and reputation.

A "BC" can be done by using public records, databases, interviews, and other sources to uncover any relevant information that may be useful for the investigation.

Private investigators use various methods and means to conduct background checks.

Some of the common techniques and resources include;

Public record searches:
Investigators access databases and records available to the public, such as court records, property records, business registrations, and motor vehicle records.

Online search engines and social media:

Investigators utilize search engines, social media platforms, and online directories to gather information about individuals, including their online presence, employment history, educational background, and associations.

Interviews and witness statements:
Investigators interview individuals who know the subject of the background check, such as friends, colleagues, neighbors, and former acquaintances.

They may also gather witness statements to corroborate information.

Surveillance:
Private investigators may conduct Surveillance on the subject to gather information about their activities, habits, and associations.

Surveillance can involve discreetly monitoring the subject's movements, documenting their interactions, and observing their behavior.

Background screening companies: Investigators may partner with background screening companies that have access to specialized databases and resources that aggregate information from various sources, including criminal records, credit reports, employment history, and educational records.

Online research tools: Investigators utilize specialized online research tools and databases that provide information on individuals, such as their criminal history, financial records, professional licenses, and court records.

Private and proprietary databases:

Private investigators may have access to exclusive databases and resources that are not available to the general public, providing them with more comprehensive information about individuals.

It's essential to note that the specific methods and resources used by private investigators may vary depending on the jurisdiction, legal requirements, and scope of the background check.

Additionally, investigators must conduct their activities within the boundaries of the Law, respecting privacy rights and following applicable regulations.

Undercover work:

Private detectives might go undercover to gather information discreetly.

Undercover work involves assuming false identities and infiltrating organizations or groups relevant to the investigation.

They gather information and build relationships while maintaining their cover to uncover valuable insights or evidence.

Interviewing and interrogations:
Private detectives conduct interviews and interrogations to gather witness statements and testimonies or to obtain information from involved parties.

They utilize their communication skills to coax information out of individuals while being mindful of legal and ethical boundaries.

Forensic analysis:
Private detectives with specialized skills may perform forensic analysis of evidence related to a case.

Forensic analysis can include examining documents, analyzing computer data, or processing crime scene evidence.

They may work closely with forensic experts to collect and analyze evidence that might be useful in solving the case.

Open-source intelligence:

Private detectives use various open-source intelligence (OSINT) techniques to gather information from publicly available sources.

OSINT can include internet research, social media monitoring, online databases, and public records searches.

OSINT is a valuable tool for efficiently collecting information, but it requires expertise to verify the authenticity and reliability of the data.

Covert operations:
In certain cases, private detectives may engage in covert operations, which involve setting up scenarios or interactions to collect evidence or gather information.

Covert operations can include placing undercover agents, using decoys, or utilizing setups to uncover the truth.

Collaboration with other professionals:
Private detectives often collaborate with attorneys, law enforcement agencies, forensic experts, or forensic accountants. Collaboration allows them to combine their skills and resources to solve complex cases efficiently.

It is important to note that private detectives must operate within legal boundaries and adhere to ethical guidelines.

PIs must respect individual privacy rights and cannot engage in illegal activities to obtain information.